Everything You Need to Know

WHEN SOMEONE YOU KNOW HAS BEEN KILLED

Although many adults shy away from the subject, talking about death is an important step toward recovery when someone you know has been killed.

• THE NEED TO KNOW LIBRARY •

Everything You Need to Know

WHEN SOMEONE YOU KNOW HAS BEEN KILLED

Jay Schleifer

THE ROSEN PUBLISHING GROUP, INC.
NEW YORK

To Cathlen and the kids, for all their help and insight.

Published in 1998 by The Rosen Publishing Group, Inc.
29 East 21st Street, New York, NY 10010

First Edition
Copyright © 1998 by The Rosen Publishing Group, Inc.

Library of Congress Cataloging-in-Publication Data

Schleifer, Jay.
    Everything you need to know when someone you know has been killed / Jay Schleifer. -- 1st ed.
         p. cm. -- (The Need to know library)
    Includes bibliographical references and index.
    Summary: Discusses death and the fear of death, explains the emotions experienced when someone you know is killed, and gives strategies to cope with them.
    ISBN 0-8239-2779-2
    1. Grief in adolescence--Juvenile literature. 2. Bereavement in adolescence--Juvenile literature. 3. Teenagers and death--Juvenile literature. [1. Death. 2. Grief.] I. Title. II. Series.
BF724.3.G73S35 1998
155.9'37--dc21
                                98-16193
                                    CIP
                                      AC

Manufactured in the United States of America.

Contents

Introduction

*B*rittany Martinez was a popular student at a small-town school in Illinois. She did not show up for class one Monday in late May. When one day stretched to two, three, and more, Brittany's friends became concerned. They were shocked to learn that Brittany's parents didn't know where she was. Nor did the police. The last time anyone had seen Brittany, she was sitting on her front porch. Then she was gone.

Within days posters were all over town, asking "Have you seen this girl?" Television news shows and newspapers from all over the state covered the story. A sign in front of the school read "Please come home, Brittany." The police said that Brittany may have run away. At least that was what everyone hoped.

That hope ended a week later when two boaters found Brittany's murdered body in the weeds on a muddy riverbank. Her killer was unknown.

The news of Brittany's death cut like a knife through the town where she lived. At school, some students were too stunned to speak. Others huddled in small groups. They whispered, wept, and clung to each other for support. The usually noisy hallways were deadly silent.

The community was in shock. Ever since Brittany's body was found, residents' fear had been growing. Had Brittany been the victim of a random kidnapping, or did she know her killer?

Students wondered if such a tragic death could happen to them, too.

Suppose unexpected tragedy happens in your community. Suppose someone you know is killed. How will you react? What will you feel? Will you be ready to help yourself and others get through it?

You'll feel many different emotions when someone you know is killed. You may feel guilty that you are still alive, grateful that you weren't the victim, stunned by the loss of someone you loved, or afraid of the dangers that you now see lurking around you. This book will help you develop the skills to deal with these emotions. It will also explain how you can help others to cope with their feelings of fear, rage, and grief.

No one is immune to tragedy. It can affect anyone at any time. However, you can learn coping skills to help you survive the trauma and grief you feel when someone you know has been killed.

Faced with a real-life death, many people wonder why they have difficulty coping when it seems so easy in movies and on television.

Chapter 1

A Taboo Topic

Despite the fact that everyone must deal with death at some point in his or her life, society does not teach young people how to cope with it. Most people don't even like to discuss it. Instead of saying that someone has died, people usually say that the deceased person has "passed on" or "passed away." They might even use the terms "expired" or "checked out." Newspapers refer to people who have died recently as "the late Mr. or Ms.," now among the "departed." Rarely does someone simply say, "They're dead."

Young people often have a special blind spot when it comes to understanding death. As a teenager, it is easy to feel as if you are going to live forever. You may feel as if you are invincible. It is hard to imagine that death can intrude on your life.

More often young people do not know how to handle death because adults do not teach them. Have you ever noticed that conversations about death and dying often stop when a child or teen enters the room? Adults may prevent young people from going to funerals and cemeteries or from viewing the body of a family member or friend. Parents take these steps in the hope of protecting their children's feelings. They have the best intentions.

However, study after study shows that young people need to know the facts about death, and they need to say good-bye to the person who has died. When she was barred from visiting the grave of a close friend, one teen set up a mini-gravesite in her room. She could place flowers on her version of the grave whenever she desired. Talking about death and attending ceremonies for the dead are not harmful to young people. Although these rituals can be upsetting, they teach you a difficult truth about life and how to cope with it. Sharing your feelings about death with other people is a way to get support for yourself.

Death, Hollywood-Style

When we see someone killed on television or in a film, it is often a cleaned-up version. Those who die of illness usually just seem to go to sleep. In other television programs and movies, death is widespread. Heroes and villains kill dozens of characters, often violently and thoughtlessly. These programs are meant to entertain. They rarely show the pain or suffering of the victim or the devastating impact of the killing on the victim's

Sharing your feelings about death with other people is a way to get support.

family and friends. Death on television or in movies is usually simpler to understand and easier to get over than it is in real life. Faced with a real-life death, people often wonder why they are having such a hard time coping when it seems so easy on television.

Famed World War II General George S. Patton knew he had to prepare his soldiers to face violent death. To get his troops ready, Patton would describe the horrors of war in full, bloody detail. Patton knew the death of someone you know raises powerful feelings. He wanted his soldiers to know what to expect when someone was killed so that they could cope with their emotions.

Far-Reaching Effects

Violent death provokes extremely powerful feelings

Unexpected deaths happen—even to those we consider invincible.
James Dean, American actor. Died in a car crash, 1955.

because it is usually unexpected and seems so sense-less. The victim does not even have to be a close friend or family member. He or she might just be someone that we see daily in a classroom, in a club, or in our neighborhood. Tragic deaths have a far-reaching effect. You are reminded about your own mortality when someone around you is killed. The world does not seem as secure or as safe as it once did. You may be sad about the death but worried about yourself at the same time. Violent death is frightening because it reminds everyone that no one is going to live forever.

People who knew someone who suffered a violent death go through a multi-step process before they can let go and continue with their lives. That process is called grieving, or mourning. Grieving is painful, but there are ways to make it easier.

Chapter 2

Tragic or Violent Death

Few people seem better protected against misfortune than Prince William, the future king of England. Yet he and his brother, Prince Harry, were awakened in the middle of the night and told that their mother, Princess Diana, had just been killed in a car crash. The lives of these two young boys, who seemingly had everything they could ever want, would never be the same.

In the weeks that followed Princess Diana's tragic death, millions of people around the globe mourned the loss of a woman who had died such a sudden, violent death.

The Worst Can Happen

These days, the chance of someone in your world suffering a violent, tragic, and unexpected death is real.

Tragic deaths have a far-reaching effect. At Kensington Palace in Great Britain, people from all around the world mourned the death of Princess Diana in 1997.

Many such deaths are the result of car accidents. According to the National Highway Traffic Safety Administration, in the United States more than 41,000 people died as a result of traffic accidents in 1996. An average of 115 people per day, or one person every thirteen minutes, died in this way.

Some teens even add to the danger that already exists. Danger thrills and excites them. They may participate in extreme sports, such as bungee jumping and ice climbing. Some take additional risks by riding motorcycles or driving cars at extreme speeds while ignoring protective equipment such as helmets and seatbelts. Also, teens who use alcohol or drugs before driving increase their chances of accidental death.

In a disaster, such as the downing of TWA Flight 800, hundreds or even thousands of people can be killed suddenly.

Freak accidents will still occur, even when you follow safety rules. The debate about the safety of air bags in automobiles shows that there are no guarantees. In fact, a device meant to protect you from harm can be the very thing that kills you. In one car crash, the vehicle's airbags opened as planned. Three of the four young people inside the car survived the accident. But the air bag slammed too hard into the fourth teen and killed her. While any accidental death is hard to understand, freak accidents are extremely disturbing because the cause of death seems so unbelievable.

Accidents are the greatest killer among young people between the ages of fifteen and twenty. More people in the prime of their lives die in car crashes, drownings, falls, and similar tragedies than from any disease, including AIDS.

'Bangers, Jackers, and Invaders

Sudden, violent death does not happen only by accident. It can be caused by a murder, a violent act, or simple carelessness. Random lawbreaking, family violence, rape, abduction, and teen gangs also can cause sudden and violent death.

Criminal gangs have existed for centuries. Members once were armed with fists or knives. Today's gangbangers pack Mac and Uzi submachine guns. Rather than fighting for ownership of a street corner, today's gang wars decide who will control millions of dollars in drug sales.

With so much at stake, drug dealers often use murder to dispose of their rivals. Often attacks occur through drive-by shootings. In a drive-by shooting, a carload of armed gang members drive by the victim and shoot at him or her from the car window. Firing from a moving car leads to poor aim, and the gang members often kill innocent bystanders, too.

Many gang members commit violent deeds in order to join the gang. To join the New York Bloods, for example, each new member has to slash an innocent subway rider with a sharp object.

Today crimes are occurring everywhere, from streets, to places of employment, to homes. In a carjacking, an auto thief jumps into a car when the victim is still at the wheel, often kidnapping him along with the vehicle. In a home invasion, armed thugs burst into a house despite the fact that the family is home. Fighting back or even crying out can provoke a deadly beating or even a bullet.

Death by the Numbers

Many of the most publicized tragedies are disasters. A disaster is a sudden event that can bring great loss of life, damage, or destruction. In a disaster, death can strike hundreds or even thousands at a time. The downing of TWA Flight 800 in 1996 killed more than 200 people, including a high school French club bound for Paris. Each year, natural disasters such as hurricanes, tornadoes, earthquakes, floods, fires, mudslides, and volcanoes kill hundreds of thousands of people and force entire nations into mourning.

Although disasters are infrequent, they often get wide TV coverage. You can see them unfolding right in your living room. Sometimes the pictures and reports are so vivid that you can feel the pain of loss just as if you were there. Up-to-the-minute reports of devastating disasters make the world seem scarier and more dangerous for everyone. Suddenly, it seems as if no one is safe from sudden or violent death.

Chapter 3

The Grieving Process: First Feelings

The first day you learn of a death is the day you begin a process called mourning or grieving. This process happens because, when someone dies, human beings need time to adjust to the changes it brings.

Many kinds of changes occur. The death of someone close can have a tremendous emotional impact. You become involved with the people you love. You are happy when you are with them and sad when apart from them. Death means being apart forever. This takes a major adjustment.

If a parent has been killed, especially the family breadwinner, returning to a normal life may mean moving to a new home or school. The family may have less money. There will be changes in how the family shares its chores and responsibilities.

Even if the person was someone you barely knew, a fellow student in one of your classes or a neighbor you saw on the street, there will still be an effect. Life will seem a little less safe and secure.

"Carrie, who was one year ahead of me in high school, was killed nearby in a car crash when I was practicing with the track team," one former student recalls. "I didn't know her well. What struck me was the feeling that youth and sensible driving can't protect us from death. It shook up the entire team."

Everyone Grieves Differently

The steps of the grieving process are generally the same for all survivors, but everyone goes through them in their own way. There is no standard time to complete the process. It can take days, weeks, months, or even years to grieve.

Not everyone completes the grieving process. Some get to a certain step and go no further. As a result, they may never return to a normal life. Others bounce back to an earlier step even after they think they've passed it.

Remember, there are differences between a person's initial feelings after someone is killed and those feelings that come later.

Shock

When police broke the news of Brittany's death to the students, one of their first reactions was to go numb. They lost the ability to feel their emotions. This is because they were in shock.

Shock is how the body protects itself from having to deal with something very bad that may come in one

gigantic blow. Shock is like opening a water valve slowly to stop a flood from emerging. You let the water in,
but only a little at a time.

When a person is in shock, the body protects itself
by slowing down its systems. The heartbeat becomes
slower. Breathing becomes shallower. Blood flow drops.
The skin may become pale. The person may even faint.

The brain of a person in shock slows down in
the same way that the body does. He or she may stop
listening or even hearing what is being said, and
may not be able to think clearly. Everything, from
making decisions to making tea, takes more effort.
Some people describe being in shock as an experience
similar to walking around carrying a heavy
weight. The famous poet Emily Dickinson called it "the
hour of lead."

Shock can last from several minutes to several
days. In time, the body and mind will return to normal
speed. After that happens, the real work of getting
through the crisis begins.

Sickness

A major crisis can affect your health in several ways,
including shock. Survivors often report headaches and
stomach troubles. They may suffer a loss of appetite, or
they may have an increase in appetite. They may have
difficulty getting to sleep or have terrible nightmares
when they do. These effects can go on for weeks,
months, or even years.

Denial

When students heard that Brittany had been murdered, many responded with cries of "No!" "She can't be dead!" and "I don't believe it!"

This is denial. People in denial believe that if they simply say that something bad did not happen, then it really will not have happened.

In reality, it does not work. However, it's also easy to understand why people go into denial. It's another way to buy more time to adjust to the death. After all, if the bad thing did not really happen, then there is no need to deal with it.

In most cases, denial usually does not last long. While it occurs, it can keep survivors from making progress toward returning to a normal emotional state. In deaths involving a family member, denial can delay important decisions that families need to make right away about the funeral and insurance matters.

Denial becomes a more difficult problem when authorities cannot find the body of the deceased person, such as in a death at sea, during a war, or in a plane crash. Many years later, survivors may believe that a loved one is still alive.

Confusion

After someone has been killed, nothing seems to be as it should. Suddenly there are strangers in the house—police, medical workers, lawyers, and funeral directors. People stay home from work or school.

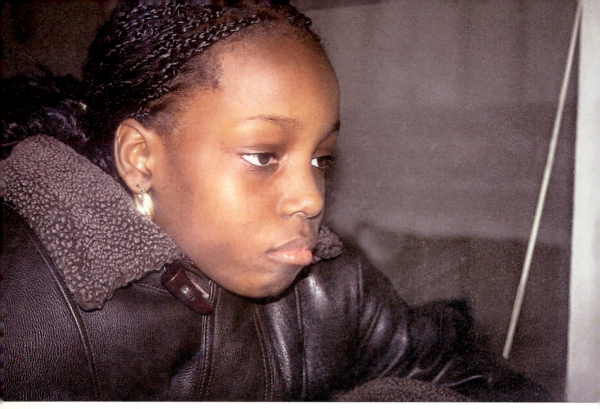

Even the death of someone you didn't know very well can make you feel less safe and secure.

No one feels able to do the shopping, cooking, and cleaning. The phone constantly rings.

When a student has been killed, the death often affects the entire school. Administrators may cancel classes, or normal teaching may give way to talks about the tragedy. Strangers, silence, and sadness rule. At such times, it's normal to feel confused and upset.

All this is temporary. The work of keeping a home, a family, or a school going will soon start up again. Life goes on.

Fear

Unexpected death can raise two kinds of fear. One concerns daily matters. When a parent, for example, dies suddenly, questions plague those left behind. Where will I live? Will I still be able to go to the same school? What will happen to me? The key to beating the panic is to realize that it takes time to answer all the questions. Don't worry, someone will answer them. Mourners need to consider these issues one at a time and try not to become overwhelmed.

The other form of fear is one for your own life. When someone dies in a violent or criminal death, people often worry that the same thing will happen to them. This fear can make a survivor change his or her style of living. After TWA Flight 800 crashed, many people canceled their plane tickets and refused to fly anymore. It was not necessary to know one of the crash victims personally. Everyone was afraid for themselves. Fear for your safety can also disturb sleep and prevent concentration on work or other important tasks.

Fighting Fear with Facts

One way to handle this fear is to learn the facts and know what your risks really are:

- Though often on television and in newspapers, deaths from criminal activity are rare. They make up only about one of every 100 deaths each year. Also, most of these result from family fights, not street or gang crime.
- Deaths in vehicle accidents are only a bit more common, about 1.3 per 100. Your chance of dying

in a plane crash is very, very slim. Only one of every 4,000 deaths happens that way. Many of those are in small, private planes, not large aircraft.

- You also can fight fear by recognizing that you are taking the proper safety steps. The police can offer ideas on how to protect yourself from crime. Signing up for a self-defense course also can help you to become less fearful.
- As for accidents, an act as simple as fastening your seatbelt in a car or wearing an approved helmet on a bike or motorcycle vastly increases your chances of surviving even a major crash. Refusing to ride with any driver who has been drinking helps even more. You can put your mind at ease by reminding others to take those safety steps, too.

Expect to Feel Shaken

The death of someone you know, even if you did not know the person well, is an upsetting event. That's especially true for young people who may have little experience with death. Expect to feel shaken. One young woman recalled how an unstable student had taken a gun to her school and killed the janitor. "I did not really know either him or the janitor," she said. "Yet suddenly I felt less safe. His death put a whole new frame around how I pictured life."

Chapter 4

The Grieving Process: Later Stages

Brittany's friends probably got over the shock of her death within a few days. Other powerful, longer-lasting feelings began to take the place of shock.

You will spend the biggest part of the mourning process dealing with these feelings. You can expect to experience most, if not all, of them during the grieving process.

Anger

When bad things happen to people who do not deserve them, it seems unfair. It's natural to become angry about unfairness. This anger may be directed toward many different people.

You may become angry at:

• **Anyone that you believe may have caused the death,** even if the cause was not clearly someone's

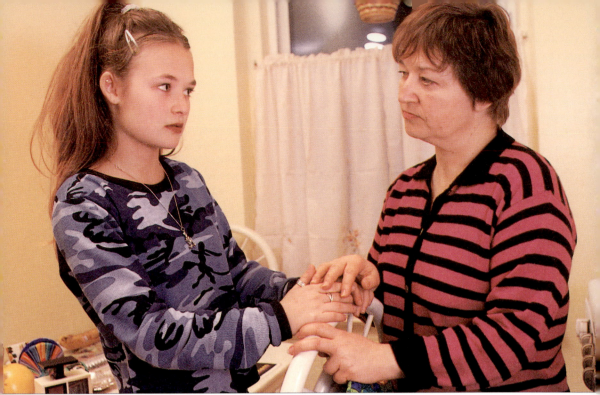
Many people do not know how to help others cope when someone is killed. You should try to be understanding and patient with those affected by a sudden, tragic death.

fault. If, for example, a car crash occurred during a terrible snowstorm, you may still blame the driver for the accident.

- **Doctors or emergency personnel.** If they were called, you may be angry at them for not being able to save the person's life. You may feel this anger no matter how hard they tried to help the person, even if the victim was too badly hurt to be saved.

- **The police and courts,** if the death was the result of a crime. Many people who have lost loved ones to crime complain that the police did not quickly catch the criminal or that the courts did not punish them severely. Some even take the law into their own hands. In one famous case, a mother entered the courtroom where the lawbreaker who had attacked her daughter was being tried. She shot and killed him. The justice system works carefully to protect everyone's rights. Unfortunately, that also means that it may work slowly.

In recent years, courts are paying more attention to the rights of victims' families. Trials happen more quickly. Also, families can now make impact statements to judges saying how their loss has affected them and what punishments they would like to see imposed upon the criminal.

- **Friends and relatives** for not saying or doing the right thing to help you. They may tell you that everything will be okay when you know it will not. They may tell you to be strong when you really need to lean on others. Many people do not know how to help others cope when someone is killed. It is important for everyone to communicate their needs clearly and to be patient with each other.

- **Yourself** for all the things you would have done differently if the person were still alive. You may also blame yourself for not spending time with or paying enough attention to the deceased person. Perhaps you now think you should have been friendlier to him or her or learned more about the person.

- **The deceased person** for leaving you in this terrible situation or for cheating you both of the good times you would have had together.

- **God or fate** for letting this happen.

When anger strikes, experts on the mourning process have this advice: give in to it, but not in a way that hurts other people. "Let it burn itself out," says Earl Grollman, the author of twenty books on dealing with death and other crises. According to him, you should try to "go for a walk, scream in private places, beat a pillow with a tennis racquet."

If others caused the death, experts caution survivors not to take the law into their own hands or to try to get even. Desiring revenge is a normal response when someone is killed, but acting on that desire is harmful to yourself and to others. Taking the law into your own hands only leads to more suffering.

What if you are angry at God or at fate? "Don't worry," says Grollman. "God can take it!"

Relief

This emotion occurs when the person who has been killed has led an especially troubled life, has been in pain, or has caused severe problems for others. The relief and the idea that "it's better this way" often are mixed with guilt about feeling something positive about someone's death.

Guilt

Most people feel some guilt about the death of someone they knew. They think of all the things they could have done or should have done. They relive the death over and over again in their minds, tormenting themselves with it.

It's natural to wonder if there was anything you could have done to prevent someone from being killed. People ask themselves questions like "Why did I let her drive after I knew she had been drinking?" or "Why didn't we go to the police for protection?" If they were part of the tragedy, they wonder why they survived and someone else did not. They wonder "Why didn't I die, too?" Often there are no answers.

Of course, all the "could have dones" and "should have dones" in the world cannot bring someone back. At best, you can learn from your mistakes. Nothing can be gained by tearing yourself apart about something that you cannot change. It is better to use the energy remembering all the fun things you did together and building for the future.

There is also another reason for feeling guilty when someone is killed. When death occurs, most people feel a certain relief that they were not the victims themselves. Soldiers have actually reported experiencing a moment of joy as enemy fire killed the troops in the next foxhole. They then immediately blamed themselves for feeling good at such a tragic time. They were not happy about the deaths, of course. They were celebrating their own survival, not someone else's death. They could not control this feeling of self-preservation. There is no reason to feel guilty if you have experienced it, too.

Fear

Fear can last long after your initial feelings of shock and confusion have ended. If the person was killed during an activity you two shared, such as a sport, you may be fearful of continuing it. Of course, death caused by violence is one of the greatest causes of fear. You may be afraid that the killer is still loose and could be after you. As mentioned earlier, many people's fear of being killed by a criminal is far greater than the chances that it actually will happen. However, if you really believe that you are in danger, share this concern with your parents and the police immediately.

You even may feel afraid after someone you do not know has been killed. Any tragedy, especially a very violent one, shows you that the universe is a scary and unpredictable place. Your life is subject to forces outside your control. No one is immune to violence, tragedy, or pain. After someone is killed, survivors have to confront their own mortality. This is a frightening thing to do.

Loneliness and Loss

Loneliness and loss are the most common emotions experienced after someone close to you has been killed. Feelings of loss take many different forms. Earl Grollman has created a list of them:

You may imagine the death over and over again in your mind. You even may feel guilty for escaping or surviving tragedy.

- **Loss of security.** If the person was a parent or other guardian, you may no longer be sure that you will always have a place to live or that your basic needs will be met.

- **Loss of faith.** You may suddenly no longer believe in God or another higher power the way you once did.

- **Loss of opportunity.** All the things that you and the deceased person might have done together will never happen. You may avoid activities that you think might lead to your own death.

- **Loss of trust.** You may believe it is no longer safe to let yourself love others. At any moment, they

might die, too. You may lose trust that the places you
visit and the people you meet are safe.

- **Loss of identity.** Confused by new and powerful
  feelings, you may believe that you really do not know
  yourself. You may doubt your ability to be the
  person you want to be.

You may retreat from life as a result of your feelings
of loss. Friends may no longer hear from you, and you
may withdraw from your family. You may put
less effort into school or work and therefore get less out
of them. You may give up enjoying today and
dreaming about your future. In the end, withdrawing
from your friends, family, and school activities
only leaves you feeling worse. You need other people
around you in order to help you deal with your loss and
your loneliness.

Grief

Grief, quite simply, is emotional pain. This pain will
be worse at first and stronger at some times than
others. Nights may be especially painful when you
are alone or have some quiet time to focus on your
feelings and memories. Grief comes and goes. In time,
though, it will completely disappear.

Moving Beyond Grief

The mourning process may be long and complicated.

Many powerful emotions will take hold of you. It takes time for these emotions to lessen and finally leave for good. However, there are some steps that you can take to help you to begin to heal.

Chapter 5

The Path to Healing

When Brittany Martinez died, many students attended the funeral and planned ways to honor her memory. In doing so, they took important steps toward healing the hurt that survivors feel when someone has been killed.

Some adults try to keep young people from dealing with death to protect their feelings. Experts say that's the wrong thing to do. The mourning process occurs at a time when you are diving into yourself and your feelings. You have to go all the way to the bottom of your emotions. There, you can start to climb back up and begin to feel well again. This process needs to unfold after any death, whether the person has died of natural causes or whether they have been killed. Here are some steps experts suggest to help you through the mourning process.

Coping With Grief

1. First and most important, let yourself feel sadness, anger, and even happiness as you recall the time you spent with the deceased person.

   Mourning brings a series of emotional ups and downs that can change from moment to moment. You cannot prevent this, and it is not healthy to try to do so. Ignore anyone who tells you to stop crying, to get over your sadness, or to be strong. Instead, be yourself! As one expert observes, "You have to recognize that you have these feelings before you can deal with them." Let the feelings out!

2. Talk about your feelings. Once you allow yourself to feel all the sorrow, rage, fear, guilt, and other emotions buried deep inside you, you need to talk about them with someone you trust. These emotions may be too tough to handle by yourself, and you will want to share them. Many people find it helpful to talk with a close family member or friend.

   If you do not have someone like this in your life, or you do not feel comfortable talking with him or her, go to a school guidance counselor, teacher, or coach. Religious leaders often are very helpful and comforting when dealing with death. Finally, crisis hotlines, such as the ones listed at the back of this book, are open twenty-four hours a day if you need someone with whom you can talk right away.

Do not be afraid to ask questions about death. Secrets and lies can prevent people from coping with death and its consequences.

3. Watch your health. When people are under stress, they are more vulnerable to health problems. Dealing with death is one of the greatest stresses in life. How do you stay well? Get rest, eat a balanced diet, and take care of your body. People in mourning tend to forget routines such as eating regular meals or getting enough sleep. It's also a good idea to get a checkup from your doctor. Tell the doctor about the death so he can appropriately treat you. Also, exercising regularly can help reduce stress. Simply going for a walk every day can help you to feel better.

4. Ask questions about the death. Most experts agree that a young person has a right to know what has

happened when someone dies. Adults may avoid telling you the truth to protect you, especially in a case when someone is tragically killed. Lies and secrets prevent people from really dealing with death and slow down the healing process.

5. Avoid alcohol. Alcohol is a depressant; it slows down the body and mind. It can increase feelings of sadness and despair. The escape from pain that alcohol abuse offers is only a temporary one. Dulling your emotions impedes the grieving process.

6. Take part in the funeral or memorial ritual if you were close to the deceased person. For example, you can give ideas for the eulogy (the speech someone makes in memory of the deceased) or help choose the music for the ceremony.

There are important reasons for being involved in these plans. Helping will keep you busy. It also will make you feel closer to others involved. Equally important, taking part in the ritual will help you to realize that the person's life is over. Mental health experts call this step closure. Why do you need this?

Many people cling to feelings of hope during tough times. Even when you know someone has died, a small part of you may believe that he or she is not really gone forever. You may think that it is just a bad dream or that some miracle will undo what has hap-

Bill of Rights
for Grieving Children

Duane Weeks, a social worker who specializes in helping young people handle grief, has put together the following *Bill of Rights for Grieving Children.*

You have a right to:

- your own feelings;
- be comforted;
- get continued loving care, though you need to understand getting care at this time may be difficult;
- help plan the funeral rites;
- get honest answers to your questions;
- be treated as important, and not as "just a kid";
- grieve for as long as it takes;
- not be expected to pick up the identity of a dead sister or brother;
- be free from guilt, and to get counseling if you need or want it;
- be a comforter to others.

pened. You cannot move on in your life while these thoughts remain. Taking part in a ceremony, being present at the burial, or viewing the person's body will help you to accept that the death is final. Then you will know that it is time to move on.

7. Make your own memorial. There are many ways to mark and honor someone's death and the life he or she lived. Among them:

   • write a story or a poem
   • compose a song
   • create a drawing or other artwork
   • make a memory book of subjects and objects the deceased person loved in life
   • review and collect photos or videos
   • light candles
   • plant a shrub, tree, or flowers
   • visit someone else suffering from the death, especially if that person is now alone

8. Join a support group. Sharing your pain and experiences with other people who really understand can be a huge step toward healing. You will learn more about support groups later in this chapter.

9. Consider your schoolmates a second family that can support you.

   If you have had to miss school because of the death, you may fear returning. You may wonder what

Jewish families may honor the lives of deceased relatives by lighting a *yahrzeit* candle.

people will think of you. Will they treat you differently? Will you be able to control your feelings in front of everyone? Will you be able to enjoy friends and activities in the way that you once did?

Other young people can be wonderfully supportive of a friend in mourning if they know that you are struggling. Let school officials know in advance the date you are returning. Then don't be afraid to ask your friends and teachers for support. They probably want to help you, but are waiting for you to tell them how to do it.

10. Understand that there are times, such as holidays, the birthday of the deceased person, or the anniversary

of the death, when you may have to deal with the sadness, grief, and fear all over again. The best way to handle this is to plan these days in advance. Light a candle or visit with family or friends to honor the person. Also, do something special for yourself. See a movie or plan something fun with your friends. Take time to remember the deceased person but take care of yourself, too.

11. Give your pain time to mend. "Time heals all wounds" might be an old saying, but, in most cases, it is true.

Support Groups in Schools

While police searched for Brittany's killer, the students at her school were on their own search. They were looking for comfort, understanding, and peace of mind.

Many schools have a process for handling tragedies and helping students cope with death. Here's how a typical program works.

1. Teachers, counselors, and the administrators quickly learn about a tragedy. A pre-established network of phone numbers is used to pass the information to each other.

2. The facts of the death are written down. Copies are given to all teachers, who then read them to all students at the same time. Students can be sure that this information is fact, not gossip.

3. In most cases, the class schedule continues normally. However, each teacher is free to use class time to discuss the event if he or she feels it would be helpful.

4. The school sets up a Crisis Room, staffed by the school nurse, guidance counselor, local religious leaders, or other professionals. This crisis team encourages troubled students to talk about the death; about all their feelings of fear, guilt, and anger; the funeral plans; and any other matters that may concern them.

5. School officials and student leaders discuss how to honor the person who died.

6. The danger signs of severe grief sometimes do not appear right away. The school contacts every student who made use of the Crisis Room each week for the next ten to twelve weeks to see how each one is feeling.

"The important thing is to . . . talk it out as soon as possible," says social worker Jeffrey Ciffone. "Then you have fewer problems later." If your school does not have an established grief program, speak to a teacher or guidance counselor about starting one. The organizations listed at the back of this book may be able to help you.

Other Support Groups

Many support groups for grieving young people also exist outside of schools. Churches, religious groups, hospitals, or mental health organizations often offer support groups. There are even teen grief support groups on the Internet. One example is the Teen Grief Conference, run by the Bereavement Education Center. Students can post their feelings, chat, or send e-mail. Some of the subjects discussed on this web site include: how relationships change after a death, continuing with school after a death, helping a friend after a death, losing a parent, losing a brother or sister, and suicide.

Support groups work by bringing together students affected by a death and having them meet weekly, every two weeks, or monthly to share feelings and experiences. Often the leaders are young people who have gone through the grief process themselves.

There are even summer camps to help young people heal. During their four-day stay at Camp Courage in Volo, Illinois, young people plant trees in tribute to their loved ones and make memory boxes. They also take part in swimming and boating and have fun around the campfire. People can only deal with grief in small portions. They need to do other things, too. Spending time working, playing, and enjoying life makes it easier to deal with the grief when it comes.

Danger Signs

Finally, be aware of these danger signs that you or someone you know is not healing properly:

- thoughts of suicide
- turning to drugs or alcohol
- avoiding other people
- feeling constantly angry or tired
- feeling that life has no purpose
- suddenly acting in ways that put one's life at risk, such as driving wildly, or taking up dangerous sports that were never of interest in the past

Should these signs develop in you or in others affected by death, it is time to seek professional counseling. There are support groups for young people in mourning as well as individual grief counselors to whom you can turn. Your school guidance counselor, family doctor, or local mental health organization can help you find these resources. The end of this book also lists several support groups that can help you.

Chapter 6

Helping a Grieving Friend

You are on your way home from school when you notice that strange events are going on at your best friend's house. The driveway is full of cars, including two police cruisers and an ambulance. The shades are drawn. People you do not recognize are going in and out of the house. You have a feeling that something bad may have happened.

A phone call confirms your fear that a tragedy has occurred. Your best friend's father has been killed in a car accident. His car was run off the road by a drunk driver. You feel terrible for your friend, but you do not know what to do.

You want to help, but what can you do? What can you say? Should you stay out of the way during such an emotional time? Should you act as if nothing has happened when you see your friend?

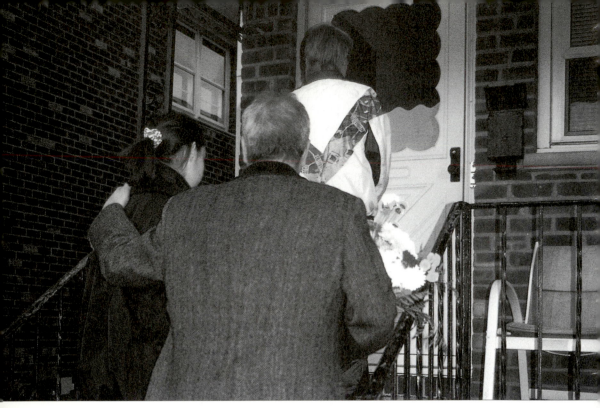

There is no "right thing" to do if you wish to help someone who is grieving. Often, your presence alone is enough.

Some Advice from Experts

- Be there. It is hard to know what to do or what to say when someone has been suddenly and tragically killed. However, you can be of no help at all if you are not there. More important, you do not want your friend to feel that you are uncomfortable with her, or that she cannot count on you in tough times. If your friend wants to be alone, she will tell you that. If she does, respect her wishes. Try not to take them personally.

- Help with the simple tasks. People in the first stages of grief tend to have trouble focusing on day to day chores. They have more important things than homework, laundry, and dirty dishes on their minds. Offer to do these tasks for them, or simply do them without being asked. Get your friend's homework assignments from his teachers or bring his books home to him if he is absent from school.

• Listen rather than talk. Let your friend do the talking. Don't be afraid to talk honestly about the death if that's what the person wants. She may want to tell stories about the deceased person. Or, she just may chat about routine matters as if nothing has happened. Let the grieving person lead the conversation.

• How should you answer when a friend in mourning expresses anger or pain? Grief support counselor Diane Fisher suggests the following list of what to say and what not to say:

What to say:
"I'm sorry."
"I care."
"I know you're hurting."
"I wish I could share your pain."
"I'm here for you."

Avoid saying things such as:
"Be strong!"

Your friend may not seem like himself after a tragedy has occurred.

> "It's God's will."
> "At least he didn't suffer."
> "She's in a better place now."
> "Don't cry."
> "You'll get over it."
> "It could have been worse."

You need to give the person time to let his emotions out. Sometimes, it is too early in the grieving process to try to make him feel better. The best thing you can do is be supportive and understanding. Sometimes, advises Fisher, a simple hug says what you need to say better than any words can.

- Let others know. You can serve an important role by letting other friends know that someone has been killed. This will help them to prepare themselves for your friend's grief.

  Carrying this news also means carrying a serious responsibility. Dramatic events, such as when someone is killed, are commonly a source of rumors and exaggerations. People add more drama to the story as they pass it from one to another. Tell only the facts that you know are true, and make them as simple and plain as possible to help squelch rumors. Also, be sensitive. Your friend may not want some details revealed. Respect her privacy.

- Most of all, understand that your friend is not going to be herself for some time. It could take weeks, months, or even years. Be patient with her mood swings and other signs of emotional upset. Both your friend and your friendship will be stronger for it in the long run.

Chapter 7

Learning to Live Again

When someone you know is killed, the pain, loss, fear, or rage can overwhelm you. It hurts, but it will not last forever. Here are a few things that you should remember that can make it easier to deal with sudden, tragic death.

Helping the Process Along

- Let your emotions out. It's usually a mistake to try to bury them or to act as if nothing has happened.

- Get the facts about the death and find out what the real risks are of dying in the same way.

- Take part in marking the deceased person's life. Attend the funeral. Talk about the person's

Many young people choose to share their feelings, fears, and personal experiences in a support group with other teens.

achievements with others. Make a memorial. Help the grieving family. You may find that the best way to make yourself feel better is to help others.

• Take safety steps to protect yourself and those you love. Such steps might include training for self-defense or simply fastening your seatbelt when you get into a car. If you really want to make a difference, you can consider joining a group that will prevent other deaths. For example, Students Against Destructive Decisions (SADD), formerly Students Against Drunk Driving, originated because young people who had lost loved ones to drunk drivers wanted to help save others from a similar fate.

If nothing else, death may give you further reasons to appreciate the beauty and joy of life.

• Let others help you feel good about life again. Many teachers, religious leaders, and mental health counselors are trained to assist people in dealing with tragedy. Almost every adult you know has had to deal with death and has learned lessons in how to do it. Don't be ashamed or afraid to ask for help.

Grieving is a series of steps, and eventually it will end. You will move beyond grief and resume living your life normally. You will not be fearful forever. Many people and organizations exist that can help you deal with your emotions. Have hope. Things will get better.

Finally, death gives you a reason to appreciate how wonderful life is. People who have survived someone being killed often never take their lives for granted again. They appreciate every moment and seek to make it worthwhile.

As one grief counselor said, "When you learn to live with death, you also learn to live."

Glossary

carjacking   A crime in which an auto thief gets into a vehicle with the victim still at the wheel. The driver often is kidnapped when the car is stolen.

closure   Completion of a process, such as finally accepting someone's death so that you can go on with your life.

counselors   Mental health professionals, such as psychiatrists and psychologists.

Crisis Room   Special area set up in a school. Students who are extremely upset due to a tragedy can get counseling here.

deceased   The person who has died.

denial   Refusal to admit that something bad, such as the death of a loved one, really has happened.

disaster   An event such as an earthquake, flood, or fire that causes great destruction, the loss of life, and many injuries.

emotions   Feelings such as happiness, guilt, relief, and sadness.

eulogy   Speech usually made by someone at a funeral to remember the life of the deceased person.

fatal   Causing death.

grief   The painful feeling that people experience when someone has died.

grief counseling   Helping people cope with their emotions after someone has died.

grieving   Expressing sadness and feelings of loss at someone's death. Also called mourning.

grieving process   Series of feelings people go through after someone's death. Also called the mourning process.

home invasion   A crime in which a thief breaks into a home while people still are in the house.

impact statement   A speech that a crime victim gives during a trial to the judge, telling how the crime has affected him or her and what punishment he or she would like imposed.

memorial   Work of art, such as a painting, poem, or song, honoring a person who has died. Also a special ceremony remembering the person.

mourning   Expressing sadness and feelings of loss at someone's death. Also called grieving.

mourning process   Series of feelings people go through after someone's death. Also called the grieving process.

shock   A slowing of the body's systems that occurs when a person suffers an injury or hears extremely bad news.

support group   Group of people formed to share
   feelings and help each other. The leader may be a
   mental health professional or someone who has gone
   through a similar experience.

Where to Go for Help

Boys & Girls Clubs of America
1230 West Peachtree Street Northwest
Atlanta, GA 30309
(404) 815-5700
Web site: http://www.bgca.org

Compassionate Friends
P.O. Box 3696
Oak Brook, IL 60522-3696
(630) 990-0010
e-mail: tcf_national@prodigy.com

Impact Personal Safety
Information on self-defense programs
(800) 345-5425

**National Directory of Children's Grief
Support Systems**
P.O. Box 86852
Portland, OR 97286
(503) 775-5683

Youth Crisis Hotline
(800) 448-4663

In Canada

YouthLink
(416) 922-3335

Also see these sites on the Internet:

Grief, Loss & Recovery
http://www.erichad.com/grief

GriefNet
Sponsored by the Rivendell Foundation of Ann Arbor, MI
http://rivendell.org/

Teen Age Grief (TAG)
http://www.smartlink.net/~tag/index.html

Teen Grief Conference
Sponsored by the Bereavement Research Council
http://www.bereavement.org/teen.htm

For Further Reading

Bode, Janet. *Death Is Hard to Live With: Teenagers Talk about How They Cope with Loss.* New York: Delacorte Press, 1993.

Bratman, Fred. *Everything You Need to Know When a Parent Dies.* Rev. Ed. New York: Rosen Publishing Group, 1995.

Buckingham, Robert, and Sandra Huggard. *Coping with Grief.* Rev. Ed. New York: Rosen Publishing Group, 1993.

Chelsea House Staff. *Death and Dying.* New York: Chelsea House Publishers, 1997.

Dockrey, Karen. *Will I Ever Feel Good Again: When You're Overwhelmed by Grief and Loss.* Grand Rapids, Minn.: Fleming M. Revell Company, 1994.

Gravelle, Karen, and Charles Haskins. *Teenagers Face to Face with Bereavement.* Englewood Cliffs, N.J.: Julian Messner, 1989.

Grollman, Earl A. *Straight Talk About Death for Teenagers.* Boston: Beacon Press, 1993.

Heegaard, Marge Eaton. *Coping with Death & Grief.* Minneapolis, Minn.: Lerner Publications Company, 1990.

Linn, Erin. *150 Facts About Grieving Children.* Incline
    Village, Nev.: The Publisher's Mark, 1990.
Moe, Barbara. *Coping When You Are the Survivor of
    a Violent Crime.* New York: Rosen Publishing
    Group, 1995.
Spies, Karen. *Everything You Need to Know About
    Grieving.* Rev. Ed. New York: Rosen Publishing
    Group, 1997.

Index

About the Author

Jay Schleifer is former editor of *Know Your World Extra*, a national classroom publication for teenage students. He has written more than forty books for teens. He is currently a publishing consultant and freelance author. He lives in the midwest.

Photo Credits

Cover by Les Mills; pages 2, 8, 24, 33, 38, 42, 48, 50, 53, 54 by Les Mills; page 11 by Ethan Zindler; page 12 courtesy of FPG International; page 15 courtesy of The Viesti Collection; page 16 courtesy of Archive Photos; page 28 by Miake Schulz.